A Tribute To John Denver

Poems, Prayers & Promises

Javana M. Richardson

StarsEnd Creations
Colorado

A Tribute To John Denver
Poems, Prayers & Promises
Published by
StarsEnd Creations
8547 East Arapahoe Road #J224
Greenwood Village, CO 80112

Copyright October 12, 1998 by Javana M. Richardson

Jacket and book design Javana M. Richardson
Cover Painting Fonda Downs

Library of Congress Catalog Card Number: 98-90386

First Edition
ISBN 1-889120-53-7

Printed in the United States of America on acid-free, elementally chlorine-free paper. As a publisher, StarsEnd Creations works to produce books of fiction and non-fiction on environmentally friendly paper and other products. Nothing is as important as the furthering of mankind in a safe and healthy environment.

Proceeds from this book will be donated to John Denver's favorite charities: The Windstar Foundation, Plant-It 2000, The Hunger Project, The National Wildlife Federation, The Cousteau Society.

To the family and friends of John who steadfastly stood by him in times good and bad. A difficult period it's been for all, yet it was such a joy to have him here all the while. It is this joy of life that we wish to celebrate.

The author of this book wishes to make it known that she is and has always been a fan of John's music and values and shares in his love for life, music, and our environment.

John's causes, founding of charitable organizations and work for the good of all are as important and enriching as any other cause that so many have donated time and resources to. It is hoped that this book will help in some small way to continue John's generous efforts and give something back to a man who gave so much to us all.

John, we know you are in a blissful and beautiful place where your music lives on and your generosity for those less fortunate ascends you to a lofty and rewarding position. Far Out.

Peace, Love and God Bless.

Acknowledgements and Contributions

BookCrafters has generously given a discount of 20% on the print run of this book. The equivalent dollar value of that discount will be donated directly to Plant-It 2000 to be used in their tree planting and reforestation efforts around the world. Thank you BookCrafters.

CONTENTS

INTRODUCTION

Well, here I am, in a place I didn't really know existed, a place where it really is possible to see the true beauty in the wilderness, in the world that surrounds us, in the vivid colors of life. I never thought it possible, as I've always been so engrossed in practical things; computer systems, pagers, housework, shopping, laundry, paying bills, survival. Now I know different.

This book began a short time ago, in March 1998, in fact. I was in the mountains—how fitting—taking a short vacation at the lovely Romantic RiverSong Bed & Breakfast in Estes Park, Colorado. Sitting in a room with a beautiful view of the trees, the snow-capped mountains, the wilderness, and with a gentle melody playing in the background, I began to feel the stress of everyday life seeping from my soul.

Contemplation can be a very interesting experience. All sorts of things pop into one's mind, and for the first time in my life, thoughts I never knew I ever knew, began to come to me. As I look back on it, it seems like some kind of connection was in the works, but from where to where, I wasn't sure.

After a time sitting and staring at that beautiful wilderness, I picked up a pen and a small notepad I had brought with me for the purpose of work (I know, I shouldn't go on vacation intending to work) and began to write. I wrote furiously, I cried, I read what I had written, I wrote some more, I read, I laughed. This roller coaster ride went on for over two hours. It was only after I felt that I could put the pen down, did I realize what I had done. More than twenty verses, lyrics or poems were on the pages of my notebook, written as if they had been dictated to me. By some miracle, they looked to be pretty good!

After re-reading them—crying and laughing all the while—I realized that they were verses and song lyrics. More important than that, I realized that they were about, around or dedicated to John Denver. Where all this came from, I'm still not sure, a gift, possibly. I had always been a fan of his, but not what one might call "a good fan". I never attended a concert, donated to his causes, asked for an autograph. I had, as I'm sure millions have, listened to his music, connected with the words and the melody, and was truly uplifted by every song I heard.

John was a man who gave everything he could to every life he touched. He inspired so many of us to work toward a better world, to be gentle with the earth, to live life to the fullest, to believe in ourselves. He was right, "one person can make a difference", and he continues to do so even now.

In listening to John's musical rendition of his life, his words (on his television shows and in his writings) and his honest assessment of life, I realized his influence on me was much more than just a passing fad. It's not something that's trendy and lasts only a short time. It's made a real difference in how I feel about my life, my family and the real reason for being here and taking this journey though life.

Since writing the verses contained in this book, I've been driven by a desire to keep John's memory and the causes so dear to him alive while at the same time, developing my own sense of charity and contribution. I've experienced a great sense of joy and fulfill-ment. I've visited the Windstar Land Conservancy in Snowmass, Colorado were I found there a true sense of beauty and love. There, I felt a real sense of togetherness and inspiration which gave me a better under-standing of the reason John was here and what he hoped to accomplish. Recently I joined an organization called Zonta, a world wide service organization of executives in business and the professions working together on charitable projects with such groups as UNIFEM and UNICEF.

This tribute is offered in loving memory and with great humility. I can never profess to be the talented and big-hearted person John Denver was, but I can certainly aspire to be a better person and try to make a difference while I'm still here. I hope you find peace and love in this tribute and remember fondly the joy that John Denver brought to this world.

- Javana M. Richardson

P.S. Thank you to the the Deutschendorf family for the beautiful card. I'll treasure it always.

Thank You's

I wish to send my most sincere and heartfelt thank you to Mr. Michael Thau of Plant-It 2000 for making the time to have lunch with me and for providing me with such a warm welcome as well as his donation to this book. Thank you to Jeanie Tomlinson for letting me visit the Windstar Land Conservancy during the Spring '98 volunteer weekend when she really had her hands full. My time there was such a warm and lovely few hours. Thank you to Jeananne Wright and her 1998 4th grade class for sharing the beautiful quilt they created and all the information surrounding the *Evening With John Denver*. Thanks to Sierra Camarena, whose story is wonderfully moving.

I've received donations of time, a place to stay, information, inspiration, warmth, support, poetry and love from the following: Kim Stachowski of The Sardy House in Aspen, Karen D'Attilo, Dr. Corie Campbell of The Daystar Commission, Michael C. Daniels and my family, Nichole Downs, Jennifer Maybury, Javana Grissam and my wonderful husband, David J. Richardson.

A special thanks to Fonda Downs for creating and donating the beautiful painting of John that graces the front cover of this book.

Last, but not least, thank you forever to Mr. Henry John Deutschendorf, Jr., John Denver, for the wonderful memories, music and the beautiful fulfilling experience I've enjoyed while writing this book.

TIME TO SAY GOODBYE
by Michael Craig Daniels

For many years we listened to
Your words and melodies,
Thanks to you we find ourselves
With dreams and memories.

Your songs of Colorado
And mountains to be climbed,
Brought us to a paradise
A "higher state" of mind.

You really made a difference, John
So thank you for your time.
I may have never met you
But you're a friend of mine.

Oh no, we won't forget you, John
Though it's time to say goodbye,
The hearts and minds of all you've touched
Will keep your dreams alive!

SUCCESS

To have laughed often and loved much;
To have won the respect of intelligent persons
    and the affection of children;
To have earned the approbation of ones critics;
To have appreciated beauty;
To have found the best in others;
To have given one's self;
To have left the world a bit better, whether by a
    healthy child or a garden patch;
To have played and laughed with enthusiasm
    and sing with exhilaration;
To have known that even one life has breathed
    easier because you lived;

This is to have succeeded.

- Ralph Waldo Emerson

Javana M. Richardson

STILL YOU'RE NOT HERE

*It's raining and pouring
And still you're not here,
You made such an impact
Your ideals were so clear.*

*We took you for granted
Then you had to leave,
Such beautiful songs
It's hard to believe.*

*You left one behind
So lovely and dear,
The melody perfect
My eyes fill with tears.*

*"For You", it is called
About love and devotion,
Your finest song ever
Evokes pure emotion.*

*A song hard to hear
So moving and deep,
You wrote it for us
Forever you sleep.*

The John Denver Quilt at Zerger Elementary School, designed and created by Jeananne Wright and her fourth grade class.

A TRIBUTE

We grew up with you
You touched us all,
We miss your face
That wonderful voice.

This tribute to you
It's all I can do,
I can do nothing else
Until it is through.

The horrible news
That your plane had gone down,
Confirmations came in
Turned our smiles into frowns.

Incredible loss
The sun went away,
Realization sets in
The pain's here to stay.

The ups and the downs
Mean nothing, you know,
Only music is left
And still the tears flow.

My 4th grade class makes a quilt every year. The children have a theme that is a current topic of interest or curriculum-related. Past quilts have been: Colorado; Endangered Species; We Are the World; We Are the Children; Nine Patch Peace Quilt; Art Around the World; Oregon Trail. This year we made a memorial quilt for John Denver, starting it less than two weeks after his death in October 1997. The children did not know much about him or his music. They interviewed two people under the age of 50 and two over 50 and presented their information to the class. In addition, I played John's music in the classroom every day. They quickly learned who he was, what he stood for, and came to love his music! Wanting to make this a special tribute to John, I worked non-stop on hand quilting to finish it before New Year's Eve, which I did, a little before midnight. I learned later that December 31 is John's birthday, and then I knew why I had been so determined to finish the quilt by then!

- Jeananne Wright

THE MOURNING HOURS

I awoke this morning
Remembering your gift,
How to get past the pain
And continue to live.

The connection to the mountains
The breeze through the fields,
Will always be the legacy
Of those you helped heal.

A quilt on the wall
May grace a feather bed,
A plaque in the wilderness
Where planes fly overhead.

All part of the legacy
Created or left behind,
To keep you in our memory
And always on our minds.

Thank you for the beauty
Our eyes will ever see,
It's been wonderful knowing
You were always there for me.

MUSIC WAS ALL

The man in the mirror
He was all the rage,
Wore his pants same as you
Stepped onto the stage.

Wore his heart on his sleeve
Was humbled by the great,
Sampled life to the fullest
Didn't tolerate hate.

Life was a dream
In a beautiful hall,
When simplicity rambled on
And music was all.

Do what you love
It's the greatest of fates,
Few find out this secret
For some it's too late.

A STAR IN THE LYRA CONSTELLATION

There is a star in Lyra that has been named
for John. It's coordinates are:
18h53m.675-D38 30'

Lyra is thought to represent the harp of
Orpheus. "Lyra gave her harp to him…"
On older skymaps Lyra is represented as a
bird: Vultur, the Vulture. Together with
Cygnus, the Swan, and Aquila, the Eagle, it
is hunted by Hercules.

HAND IN HAND

Hand in hand
Your hand in mine,
I love you my dear
Think of you all the time.

From a make-shift porch
I look out to sea,
And watch boats pass by
Both you and me.

My mind's in a funk
My life's such a blur,
I miss you so much
How could this occur.

Thank you for all
It was such a great pleasure,
To work by your side
You're a national treasure.

Life is beautiful
Sometime's even fair,
Every day with you
It's like being there.

Javana M. Richardson

ASPEN GRACE

The beauty of Aspen
That contains you
Sees the wind blow
And keeps the man
Forever in our hearts.

Children, animals, dreamers
They're all better off
Having a guardian
Always at their side.

Stars in the universe
Go on twinkling
As you continue
To make it a better place.

YOUR FRIEND

He loved the sea
He loved the earth
Since even before
This great man's birth.

Took care to please
To be divine,
Drank a little bit much
The sweet cherry wine.

Loved to fly high
Played hard and played rough,
Worked many long hours
On himself he was tough.

Crying time is all but over
Move on to greater days,
And fear not the living
Your dreams will find a way.

Keep listening for music
You'll find on the wind,
A gift for tomorrow
Love always, your friend.

THIS SONG IS FOR YOU

John, we hope that you will see
You've touched our lives eternally
You'll live on in our memory
This song is for you.

Country Roads they lead *Back Home Again*
And *Grandma's Feather Bed* within
Now *Follow Me* and let's begin
Our song that is for you.

The trees they sigh your melodies
Your words are borne on gentle breeze
Like *Poems, Prayers and Promises*
This song is for you.

Guess He'd Rather be right here
In Colorado, home so dear
This Old Guitar awaits you there
This song is for you.

Rocky Mountain High, you say
Where The Eagle and the Hawk, they play
A Country Boy at heart you'll stay
This song is for you.

Sunshine on My Shoulders
Warms my heart and dries my tears
It quiets all my doubts and fears
This song is for you.

Matthew was a lucky man
To have you as a nephew, and
I'll bet he was your biggest fan
This song is for you.

Calypso on the ocean blue
And Leavin' On a Jet Plane too
You'd sing to crowds or just a few
This song is for you.

Did you ever want to *Fly Away*
Be free just like you are today
In our hearts you'll always stay
This song is for you.

Looking for Space, we know
You've found serenity and so
Goodbye Again we whisper low
This song is for you.

Jeananne Wright
1/19/98
Copyright Jeananne Wright 1998

YOU

Enough about me
It's you I'm about,
Gotta know you're okay
Wanna stand up and shout.

You're gonna make it
Through crystal clear days,
You'll see through the trees
You'll live through the haze.

Gonna come visit you
From time to time,
Wanna check on your progress
And follow your line.

You've grown and you've blossomed
It's so hard to let go,
Time's on my side
You'll continue to glow.

"John Denver's popularity since the early 1970s may be measured in record sales that few other artists have achieved, including 14 gold albums and 8 platinum albums in the U.S. alone. He has had many gold and platinum sales overseas as well, in countries including Australia, Germany and the United Kingdom. The LP "John Denver's Greatest Hits" is still one of the largest selling albums in the history of RCA Records, with worldwide sales of over 10 million copies. John Denver is one of the top five recording artists in the sales history of the music industry."

HAPPY FOR ME

*Fame and fortune's
Not what it's cracked up to be,
My life had some roses
My friend was a tree.*

*I loved my fair neighbor
Tolerated the rest,
The people were kind
That's what I loved best.*

*I have an acquaintance
Writes all my stuff down,
Didn't think me a psycho
Didn't think me a clown.*

*Watching the pain and their
Eyes fill with tears,
Makes me love all the more
Time on earth all those years.*

*Be happy for me
I've grown and desired,
I'm happy to say
It's about time I retired.*

March 22, 1998

In a tribute to the late John Denver, Aspen Skiing Company dedicated the nation's highest lift-served ski run—renamed "Rocky Mountain High"—to him, and announced that the ski lift serving the run will be powered solely by clean, renewable wind power.

INSPIRATION

Inspiration hits above the belt
It comes as no surprise,
We all have great intentions
I've seen it in your eyes.

Inspired many people
Had love as time progressed,
The mountains were endearing
The people loved the best.

Takes love and understanding
Of this I'm truly sure,
Now that you're the chosen one
I see you have the cure.

No you're not crazy
I'm here with you now,
You won't believe it
You've inspired me somehow.

"It's About Time"

I met John Denver at Windstar in 1986 when he and Tom Crum were working on a multimedia presentation having to do with the nuclear arms race. A man from Holland by the name of Fred Matser, helped fund the presentation, which allowed those who wanted to help with the project work full time with John and Tom. My husband and I volunteered and moved to Snowmass. We spent time developing the program and traveling with John and Tom around the U.S. We also went to the Soviet Union to spread the word. I spent some time on stage with John during this very moving presentation to the people. At the conclusion of these presentations, John would stand on stage and sing "I Want to Live". There wasn't a dry eye in the house. The message was clear, "stop the nuclear arms race, we all want to live". It was a busy and fulfilling time, we hiked to the mesa behind Windstar, we had picnics and we worked hard. John was so compassionate and looked you in the eye when he spoke. One day my child fell off a swing at a picnic and John ran over and picked him up and comforted him. He was such a comforting person and knew just how to make you feel warm and loved. We were one small family working to make a large contribution, helping to fulfill his dream of world peace. The project concluded in 1988. For me it was a life changing experience.

- Sierra Camarena

TELL THEM FOR ME

*Tell them they're gracious
And loving and fine,
Their lives will be touched
The way they touched mine.*

*Be there for each other
Be kind and be true,
Happiness can be found
Just as the sky's blue.*

*Constant and close
For time marches on,
My life with you always
Brought memories so fond.*

*Thank you for time
Put into my life,
You were always there for me
A wonderful wife.*

The Plaque - December 1997

There are just eight words:
"Provided by Zachary John & Anna Kate
Deutschendorf."

KNOW LOVE
(CHILDREN OF LOVE)

Your husband, he's fine
The love of your life,
He'll always be with you
He's glad you're his wife.

Life's no bed of roses
But the two shall share,
A life of salvation
He'll always be there.

Time moves on
In mysterious ways,
Find beauty in starlight
And long summer days.

Flowers of such beauty
They're coming, they'll bloom,
On rich fields of love
And snowflakes in June.

Find time for each other
Your garden to sow,
Continue to plant it
This love you shall know.

Jeananne Wright, Karen D'Attilo and Ms. Wright's
4th grade class at Zerger Elementary

Because we had so many wonder-ful responses to the quilt, we decid-ed to have an "Evening With John Denver" on February 26th, at our school, Zerger Elementary. About 325 people were in attendance. Several of John's friends where there also. One of them, Karen D'Attilo, adopted my class and worked many hours with us plan-ning and preparing for the evening. She and John led children's choirs together in Aspen. She had my kids singing their hearts out! I was especially pleased when the evening arrived and John's moth-er, aunt and cousin walked into the hallway and asked directions to the gym. She had read about the "Evening" in the morning newspaper. John's friends, our PTA president, Gregg Greenstein and I played our guitars, sang, and accompanied my class in many of John's songs. Afterwards John's mother said that the evening was one of John's greatest memorials. It was a wonderful and magical night.
- *Jeananne Wright*

PLEASE DON'T CRY

Don't know when I'll be back
I know I'll see you soon,
You see I have a plane to catch
I'm headin' to the moon.

Those who are close to me
Should never forget,
For you I'll always be there
I have no real regrets.

OK, I hear you clearly
You're begging me to stay,
You know that it's not possible
But you ask it anyway.

I'll love you all forever
On this you can count,
Forever's a long, long time
I'll see you all around.

JUST KEEP ON GOING

An incredibly talented underdog
Has both bad days and good,
Not always treated poorly
Just usually misunderstood.

Working is hard
The demands overlooked,
Just keep on going
Be a short order cook.

Relaxation comes at a price
Thoughts wonder good and bad,
Emotions overtake us
The music makes us sad.

From where does inspiration come
When all is down the drain,
We're left with sad devotion
But mostly with the pain.

John played a variety of roles to me throughout my life; as close family friend, superstar, mentor and finally employer. He taught me to ski, to delegate responsibility, to care for the environment and to live life. Most of all, he demonstrated that 'one person can make a difference.' This was the most powerful teaching of all.

In the early 90's, John founded Plant-It 2000 - a nonprofit tree-planting foundation dedicated to properly planting, maintaining and protecting indigenous trees worldwide. I was selected as the Executive Director and I reported directly to John and the other Board of Directors. John would periodically call me up and give some advice or ask what types of tree-planting projects we had scheduled for the near future. Working with John professionally was certainly a different relationship than knowing him as a very close family friend.

The things that stand out most about John relate to his view of the world. He did not feel separate from the environment and constantly was empowering others to change their community, their forest or even communities and forests far away from themselves. John wanted people to do these things out of respect for being balanced - not because of his celebrity.

If my family had never met and became part of John's life, I would be less empowered to make changes in the world. After seeing in action one person's will properly applied and its effects, I have learned that we each can make our neighborhood, city, forests and most importantly, ourselves, healed.

- Michael Thau
Executive Director - Plant-It 2000

To Hell And Back

*I've been there
To Hell and back,
Sometimes it helps
To take a good snack.*

*When down and out
In Beverly Hills,
Try your hand at some garbage
It might pay the bills.*

*It's time to be serious
Time for a change,
This world's on the fast track
Take a ride on the range.*

*It takes one to know one
A cowboy like me,
I give you this message
To show you the trees.*

*They're there for enjoyment
And beautiful too,
Please care for them always
They'll be good to you.*

"John's candle grows brighter each day."

SHINE ON

Shut up and keep writing
Make something of your life,
The world's full of sunshine
And unhappy strife.

You can do anything you want
The good and the bad,
But do yourself favors
And don't be so sad.

Life on the prairie
Life on the range,
There's a light in your eyes
It all seems so strange.

The love in your day
The sun in your way,
Do what you do best
Go lie in the hay.

Javana M. Richardson

*"The future of life on Earth depends on our ability to
see the sacred where others see only the common"*
- John Denver 1991

Folks have shared numerous stories where John
expressed this thought through his actions. I am
reminded of two such occasions: The first was with
a young woman who wasn't handling our high alti-
tude very well during a Choices symposia. As
Medical Aid team leader, I called for ambulance
transport to Aspen Valley Hospital. John overheard
the conversation and without hesitation asked if he
could be of some assistance. He came to the medical tent, sat on the edge of the cot, holding this
woman's hand, talking with her in quiet reassuring
tones until the ambulance arrived. His connection
remained as he asked for updates on her condition
as the weekend unfolded. On another occasion, we
had a child who had become anxious over perform-
ing, which triggered an asthma attack. John was
close by our tent and came to her side - within min-
utes, her breathing stabilized and she went on to
perform in the Earthsavers program that afternoon.
I'm sure these two individuals cherish the connection they made with this compassionate man who
truly cared about the human family and all that sup-
ports life.

- Jeanie Tomlinson
Windstar Managing Director

SHARE THE DREAM

Mention my name
Whenever you need,
Tell them I cared
And planted a seed.

In the heat of the night
They'll continue to grow,
The lights are still on
Don't hesitate to know.

Share the dream with all
The beauty be told,
You're on to something
Creating the gold.

The platinum is there
But just within reach,
Keep upping yourself
Continue to teach.

Say what you mean
Mean what you say,
Stick to your convictions
They're not in the way.

This 36 by 24-inch bronze sculpture of John Denver hangs at Aspen's airport above a bench donated in John's memory. The bronze bas-relief was commissioned by an anonymous donor and created by Colorado sculptor, Robert Henderson. The inscription reads

1943 John Denver 1997
"Rocky Mountain High"

Behind John on the plaque is an airplane, aspen trees and the mountains he loved so much.

HEY MAN

We stood in a time
When "For" meant something.
Glad we could do it
And still keep on going.

You stayed with me always
Sometimes went for a ride,
But more often than not
You walked by my side.

There's many great people
Watch out for the flames,
They'll lick at your boots
And teach you their games.

All in all
Never forget,
Life is short
Cover your bets.

Drive Carefully.

ABOUT CARS

Love 'em, love 'em a lot
Cars are like people
Look great in the lot.

Miss them a great deal
Miss the keys, miss the seats
Miss the way that they feel.

Planes and helicopters
They'll get you around,
With some experience
Should stay on the ground.

Have some great food
Wine, women and song,
Make sure to have fun
And that you go long.

Gonna stop all the silliness
Cause I know it's the rage,
To read a good book
Life starts on first page.

The passing of John Denver has touched the world and has deeply touched those of us at Windstar. His essence is felt here in this land he loved so much. As we move forward from the profound shock and grief of this loss, we are beginning to focus on the joy John has left us. He was able to connect us all soul to soul in a way that no other poet/composer has ever done. Through his music and spoken word he urged us to love one another more deeply; to honor the diversity among all life; to have respect for the splendor and fragility of our environment - his words moved us to action. John was so much more than an entertainer - he was of course a son, a brother, a father, but he was also a humanitarian and a teacher! He remains a teacher to those who will listen and hear the messages within the lyrics of his songs.

- Jeanie Tomlinson
The Windstar Foundation

ENVIRONMENTAL ISSUES

Slime in the oceans
Soot in the trees,
Watch out for the junk
In the air that you breathe.

Work hard so the children
Can continue to live,
In just the same comfort
That we always did.

We've always been guilty
Of not caring enough,
Make sure everyone
Can spend time in the rough.

Gonna take lots of effort
Bunches of work,
Gotta get your hands dirty
And clean up the earth.

"For me, John was a teacher - I think he taught us much about ourselves; to love - to be gentle with one another and gentle with the planet."

- Jeanie Tomlinson

FOR ME

Go to the mountains
Breathe in some fresh air,
You just never know
How long it'll be there.

Yes, I'm talking to you
And the person you're with,
Take some responsibility
For the land is your gift.

Remember me always
Not for fortune or fame,
But my true love of life
That won't ever wane.

Take care and consider
The oceans, the earth,
They're tender and fragile
I know what they're worth.

To love is tremendous
With feelings so free,
If not for yourself
Then do it for me.

"Music does bring people together; it allows us to experience the same emotions. People everywhere are the same in heart and spirit. No matter what language we speak, what color we are, the form or our politics or the expression of our love and our faith, music proves: We are the same."

- John Denver

THE COLOR OF MUSIC

Sensing the beauty
Lifelong and true,
Heightened each moment
Spent listening to you.

The color of music
The bright lively pace,
I'm sad at the prospect
And miss your sweet face.

You can speak with me always
Any time day or night,
I'll welcome your nearness
And watch you take flight.

I'll lift up your spirits
And give you some time,
Enriching your lifeline
The way you did mine.

I REMEMBER HIM

He wasn't really on my list
I knew he wrote some tunes,
He didn't really strike me
As someone on the move.

Don't remember the music
Just trials he's been through,
But playing his hits
"Oh yeah, I liked that one too."

We reminisce about his life
And listen to his songs,
Remembering the words
We begin to sing along.

The beautiful mountains
The fire in the sky,
The children who knew him
Didn't have to ask why.

Focusing on the bad
Not the good that's within,
His history of giving
"Oh yeah, I remember him."

John Denver receives his PhD degree posthumously from The Daystar Commission. This degree was originally to be presented to John in the Summer of 1997, but, due to unavoidable delays, that was not possible. This degree in the Humanities is for John's significant, original, personally designed and carried-out musical, literary, and humanitarian work. Copies of the degree were recently accepted by some of John's closest friends and members of the Denver family.

This is not an honorary degree; rather, it is an academic degree and a leadership degree, part of our effort to produce a shift at the doctoral-level in the entire field of the humanities so that it fosters more appropriate academic excellence and better serves the needs of humankind and the needs of the earth. The people we confer degrees on are dedicated leaders who have done the hardest and most noble hands-on work, often taking far longer and requiring more research, talent, personal

effort, dedication and sacrifice than other uni-
versity doctorates. The majority of our PhD
degree recipients are not celebrities.

As far as we know, The Daystar Commission
is the only educational institution of its kind.
What makes us unique is that we insist that the
humanities should be "for" humanity rather
than simply "about" humanity. To that end, we
are engaged in a serious effort to shift attention
at the doctoral level in the field of the humanities away from abstract theoretical develop-
ment and towards creative, substantial, and
humanitarian action within the worldwide
human community.

In order to achieve this shift, we reserve the
PhD for people who have designed and personally carried out significant creative and humanitarian projects of an enduring quality. This is
our way of acting as the machinery that drives
the academic shift in this new direction. We
want to be able to point to the kind of creative
and humanitarian work the world needs, the
kind we hope greater numbers of people will
begin to engage in. We need leaders who are
role models and mentors in this kind of work.
Conferring PhD degrees on those who clearly
have already completed the required work is
just the first step in our effort.

John Denver was a supreme example of the kind of leadership we look for in our PhD degree recipients. He was a person of vision, compassion, and understanding, a tremendous leader who did truly great projects, employing all of his wisdom as a mature human being in order to create an enduring structure of life-affirming musical, literary, and dramatic substance in the mode of compassion, including his dynamic efforts on behalf of Mother Earth.

He brought comfort and inspiration to many people all over the world, working hard to end hunger on the face of this earth. In the legacy of his music, his environmental and humanitarian efforts and permanent structures, in the records of his ideas and feelings, and in all the other marks and emblems of his life, he will continue to comfort, inspire and educate us all. We are deeply honored in the privilege of conferring upon him this degree.

- Dr. Corie Campbell
The Daystar Commission

An Example For All

Didn't matter what you looked like
Didn't matter you were there,
What mattered the most
Is how much you cared.

Your boots made for running
Didn't matter how old,
You planted your trees
All over the world.

We're really most grateful
And see what you've done,
The difference is stunning
The battles you've won.

Wanna try and do better
Find the time and the place,
To continue your work
And bask in your grace.

You've shown us the way
To walk in your steps,
Your music does lead us
And brings out the best.

DEAREST JOHN

The forest, the eagle
The sky and the ocean,
All equally received
Your love and devotion.

Devoted you were
So much that it hurt,
You sang for the people
To spread the true word.

The movies, the stories
The songs and their themes,
Opened your life up to all
And showed us your dreams.

We're glad to have known you
Your efforts tipped the scales,
You've inspired us incredibly
Put the wind in our sails.

We begin where you left off
No matter what they say,
Your goals will live on
You've shown us the way.

ALL THE BEST

It's what you gave
To all who heard,
Your music, your thoughts
Those incredible words.

The life and times
of the real John Denver,
Were just like your songs
And love's sweet surrender.

The goal always giving
You took such strides,
To make everything right
Through deep crashing tides.

I could have done something
While you were still here,
Let you know you're the difference
That made everything clear.

Now that you're home
High on that hill,
Your love, it surrounds us
Our hearts are fulfilled.

Javana M. Richardson

The Windstar Foundation and
the Rocky Mountain Institute
Snowmass, Colorado

SPIRIT OF LIFE
--For John

As I walked quickly to the door
The panic began to show,
I took a deep and cleansing breath
And knew I had to go.

I could see why he loved it
This place he called home,
The views just spectacular
The trees weren't alone.

Returning to nature
Gentle hands work the land,
Volunteers from all places
Fulfill a dream, hand in hand.

I met the managing director
And others kind as she,
I saw the pain there in her eyes
Felt the sadness deep in me.

We talked a long time
'Bout this, that, and thou,
I saw that I was welcome
The caring here and now.

SPIRIT OF LIFE
--For John (continued)

I sat on the old brown couch
With cracks and crinkles and such,
All the lumps here and there
Held your charm and your touch.

Scrapbooks on the table
Assembled with loving care,
Hold lots of your sweet memories
We all wished you were there.

Such a feeling of warm love
In this place in the woods,
I felt right at home
Every place that I stood.

When I finished my stay
They were glad that I came,
As I walked out the door
The wind whispered your name.

Written by Javana M. Richardson
During a trip to Aspen after visiting the
WindStar Land Conservancy

Letter to a fan:

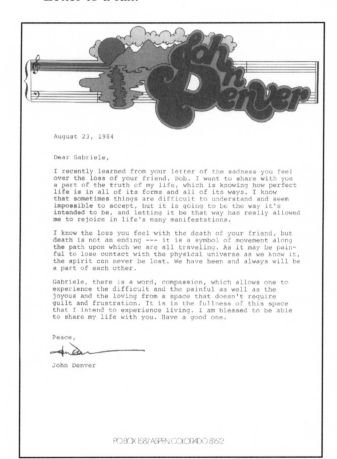

August 23, 1984

Dear Gabriele,

I recently learned from your letter of the sadness you feel over the loss of your friend, Bob. I want to share with you a part of the truth of my life, which is knowing how perfect life is in all of its forms and all of its ways. I know that sometimes things are difficult to understand and seem impossible to accept, but it is going to be the way it's intended to be, and letting it be that way has really allowed me to rejoice in life's many manifestations.

I know the loss you feel with the death of your friend, but death is not an ending --- it is a symbol of movement along the path upon which we are all traveling. As it may be painful to lose contact with the physical universe as we know it, the spirit can never be lost. We have been and always will be a part of each other.

Gabriele, there is a word, compassion, which allows one to experience the difficult and the painful as well as the joyous and the loving from a space that doesn't require guilt and frustration. It is in the fullness of this space that I intend to experience living. I am blessed to be able to share my life with you. Have a good one.

Peace,

John Denver

P.O. BOX 1587 ASPEN COLORADO 81612

Courtesy Gabriele Gramaglia

INSTRUCTIONS FOR LIFE

1. Give people more than they expect and do it cheerfully.
2. Memorize your favorite poem.
3. Don't believe all you hear, spend all you have or sleep all you want.
4. When you say, "I love you", mean it.
5. When you say, "I'm sorry", look the person in the eye.
6. Be engaged at least six months before you get married.
7. Believe in love at first sight.
8. Never laugh at anyone's dreams.
9. Love deeply and passionately. You might get hurt but it's the only way to live life completely.
10. In disagreements, fight fairly. No name calling.
11. Don't judge people by their relatives.
12. Talk slowly but think quickly.
13. When someone asks you a question you don't want to answer, smile and ask, "Why do you want to know?"
14. Remember that great love and great achievements involve great risk.
15. Call your mom.
16. Say "bless you" when you hear someone sneeze.
17. When you lose, don't lose the lesson.

18. Remember the three R's: Respect for self; Respect for others; Responsibility for all your actions.
19. Don't let little disputes injure a great friendship.
20. When you realize you've made a mistake, take immediate steps to correct it.
21. Smile when picking up the phone. The caller will hear it in your voice.
22. Marry someone you love to talk to. As you get older, their conversational skills will be as important as any other skill.
23. Spend time alone.
24. Open your arms to change, but don't let go of your values.
25. Remember that silence is sometimes the best answer.
26. Read more books and watch less TV.
27. Live a good, honorable life. Then when you get older and think back, you'll get to enjoy it a second time.
28. Trust in God, but lock your car.
29. A loving atmosphere in your home is so important. Do all you can to create a tranquil harmonious home.
30. In disagreements with loved ones, deal with the current situation; don't bring up the past.
31. Read between the lines.
32. Share your knowledge. It's a way to achieve immortality.

33. Be gentle with the earth.
34. Pray — there's immeasurable power in it.
35. Never interrupt when you are being flattered.
36. Mind your own business.
37. Don't trust someone who doesn't close their eyes when you kiss them.
38. Once a year, go someplace you've never been before.
39. If you make a lot of money, put it to use helping others while you are living. That is wealth's greatest satisfaction.
40. Remember that not getting what you want is sometimes a stroke of luck.
41. Learn the rules then break some.
42. Remember that the best relationship is one where your love for each other is greater than your need for each other.
43. Judge your success by what you had to give up in order to get it.
44. Remember that your character is your destiny.
45. Approach love and cooking with reckless abandon.
46. Never be afraid to ask.

A PARTIAL LIST OF
JOHN DENVER'S ACHIEVEMENTS

1974 - Cashbox's #1 Album Seller and #1 Artist
- ASCAP Award for Top Album of the Year
1974/75 - Record World's Top Recording Artist
1975 - ABC'S Bi-centennial Music Award for
Top Male Vocalist by the National Press
- Country Music Entertainer of the Year
Country Music Song of the Year - *Back Home Again*
People's Choice - Favorite Musical Performer
- AGVA Singing Star of the Year
1977 - People's Choice Award
- Poet Laureate of Colorado
1979 - U.S. Jaycee's Ten Outstanding Men of
America Award
- Whale Protection Fund Service Award
1982 - Carl Sandburg's People's Poet Award
1985 - NASA Medal for Public Service
- Presidential "World Without Hunger Award"
1990 - National Wildlife Federation Conservation
Achievement Award
- International Center for Tropical Ecology
World Ecology Award
1993 - Albert Schweitzer Music Award
1997 - Songwriters Hall of Fame
1998 - Grammy Award for Best Children's Album
1998 - The World Folk Music Association Lifetime
Achievement Award
1998 - Genesis Award - *Amazon*

"During the Baltimore Oriole's game's 7th inning stretch, they still play "Thank God I'm a Country Boy" at Camden Yards. They're true fans of John's."

Western Heritage Center's National Cowboy Hall
   of Fame Award
Freedom Foundation at Valley Forge - George
   Washington Award
CINE Golden Eagle Award
American Film Festival Blue Ribbon Award
1979 - Denver International Film Festival Award
Best Outdoor Travel and Recreational Film Award
Earl D. Osborn Award
1975/76 Emmy Award - Best Musical Variety
Special

BOARD OF DIRECTORS AND
ADVISORY BOARDS SERVED ON:

Presidential Commission on World Hunger
The Windstar Foundation
The Cousteau Society
The Hunger Project
Friends of the Earth
National Space Institute
est
World Federalists Association
The Kushi Foundation
Human/Dolphin Foundation
Plant-It 2000
Music Associates of Aspen
Aspen Center for Environmental Studies
The Challenger Center
NightHawk

A few more words about charity and benevolence.

Please seek out and help those in need. Other foundations and charitable institutions that are working for the betterment of life include the Denver Music Association and the Austin Nature Center as well as many others that are in the List of John Denver's Achievements included in this book.

The Denver Music Association's mission with the John Denver Music Education Fund is to recognize the musical and non-musical contributions of John Denver and to preserve the John Denver Legacy as a Global Citizen who has enriched the lives of all the people through the power and influence of music. Operating as a separate musical entity under Our Musical Heritage, a Colorado 501c(3) non-profit organization, the JDMEF promotes musical endeavors related to concerts, written materials, and educational enhancement programs which continue to emphasize global concerns with which John Denver devoted his life, to-wit: global environmental and humanitarian awareness and Colorado. Contributions can be made to: Our Musical Heritage (JDMEF), 1165 Delaware St., Denver, CO 80204-3607.

The Austin Nature Center has received permission to erect a permanent memorial to John Denver at the Austin Nature Center, a tourist and educational facility, as well as a rescue/sanctuary facility for animals which cannot be returned to the wild. A wood carving of an eagle flying into the sunset and the words to John's song "The Eagle and the Hawk" will grace the gateway to the Birds of Prey exhibit. Contributions can be sent to: Julie Boyea, PO Box 2663, Austin, TX 78768.

Peace & Love to you, John Denver.

StarsEnd Creations

8547 E. Arapahoe Road, #J224
Greenwood Village, Colorado 80112
(303) 694-1664 or FAX (303) 694-4098
www.starsend.com

Please ship _____ copies of *A Tribute to John Denver.*
(for shipments to destinations outside of the United States, please call prior to ordering)

$18.95 per copy   _____

$ 3.00 shipping per copy (USA only)   _____

Colorado residents please add 3.8% sales tax_____

TOTAL   _____

Make check payable to: **StarsEnd Creations**

Ship To:

Name_____

Address_____

City_____

State_____ Zip _____

Bill To: (if different from above)

Name_____

Address_____

City_____

State_____ Zip _____

Please allow three weeks for delivery

ORDER FORM

Fax your order to 303-694-4098 or
Mail to: StarsEnd Creations/Pantry Press
8547 East Arapahoe Road #J224
Greenwood Village, CO 80112

TITLE	AUTHOR	ISBN	PRICE	QUANTITY
A Tribute to John Denver *Poems, Prayers & Promises*	Richardson	1-889120-53-7	$18.95	_____
Mountain Magic Cuisine *Secret Recipes of the Dude & Guest Ranches of Colorado*	Guest Ranches	1-889120-11-1	$23.95	_____
Seasoned Greetings *Holiday Fare from the Distinctive Inns of Colorado*	Distinctive Inns	1-889120-13-8	$19.95	_____
Distinctly Delicious *Favorite Recipes of The Distinctive Inns of Colorado*	Distinctive Inns	1-889120-07-3	$17.95	_____
TAKE A NUMBER *Poetry In E-Motion*	Maybury	1-889120-08-1	$10.95	_____
Leavings	P.D. Cacek	1-889120-10-3	$5.99	_____
The Star Dwarves Trilogy	Richardson	1-889120-06-5	$12.95	_____
CrackedWEB, The Book	Richardson	1-889120-03-0	$12.95	_____
Shakespeare's Confession	Para	1-889120-02-2	$19.95	_____
She Died Young	Livingston	1-889120-04-9	$8.95	_____

Date: _____ **PO #** _____

Ship to:

_____

_____

_____

Bill to (if different than above):

_____

_____

_____

Phone #: _____ **Fax #:** _____